101 Questions for Couples Journal
Fun & Playful Edition

Creative Simple Press
©Copyright 2021 Creative Simple Press - All Rights Reserved.

The content within this book may not be reproduced, duplicated, or transmitted without direct written permission from the publisher.

This book has 101 unique prompt questions with fun & playful, more laid back concept.

Each page has enough spaces for both you and your partner to fill in, divided by a thick black line in the middle of the page.

These questions are not in any order, you can answer whichever one you like first, depending on you and your partner's mood.

Kindly note that some of the questions in this book may be related to your or your partner's past experiences (first crush, first heartbreak, etc.).

Feel free to skip any of the questions that you or your partner deem to sensitive to discuss about.

DATE : _____

1. WHAT WAS YOUR FAVORITE FOOD GROWING UP?

DATE: _____

2. WHAT WAS THE FIRST ALBUM YOU EVER OWNED?

DATE : _____

3. WHAT WAS YOUR DREAM JOB WHEN YOU WERE A KID?

DATE : _____

4. WHAT'S ON YOUR BUCKET LIST THIS YEAR?

DATE : _____

5. WHAT'S SOMETHING YOU'D LIKE TO TRY DOING, BUT HAVEN'T WORKED UP THE NERVE YET?

DATE : _____

6. What would you do with your life if you suddenly became a billionaire?

DATE : _____

7. WHAT ACTIVITIES MAKES YOU FEEL THE HAPPIEST WHEN YOU'RE DOING IT?

DATE : _____

8. WHAT'S THE BEST TRIP YOU'VE EVER TAKEN?

DATE : _____

9. WHAT IS THE MOST DARING THING THAT YOU HAVE DONE TILL DATE?

DATE : _____

10. WHAT'S AN IDEAL WEEKEND FOR YOU?

DATE : _____

11. If a genie granted you 3 wishes, what would you wish for?

DATE : _____

12. IF YOU ONLY HAVE 1 DAY LEFT TO LIVE, WHAT WOULD YOU DO IN THE NEXT 24 HOURS?

DATE : _____

13. WHAT'S THE CRAZIEST JOB YOU WOULD CONSIDER TAKING?

DATE : _____

14. IF YOU HAD TO SPEND 1 MILLION DOLLARS IN ONE DAY, WHAT WOULD YOU BUY?

DATE : _____

15. ARE YOU STILL IN TOUCH WITH YOUR CHILDHOOD FRIENDS?

DATE : _____

16. WHAT'S THE MOST IMPULSIVE THING YOU'VE EVER DONE?

DATE : _____

17. WHAT IS YOUR BEST CHILDHOOD MEMORY?

DATE : _____

18. WHAT IS YOUR WORST CHILDHOOD MEMORY?

DATE : _____

19. WHAT WAS YOUR BIGGEST FEAR AS A CHILD?

DATE : _____

20. WHAT IS THE SINGLE MOST IMPORTANT THING YOU LEARNED AS A CHILD?

DATE : _____

21. WHAT EVENTS ARE ON YOUR BUCKET LIST FOR NEXT YEAR?

DATE : _____

22. DO YOU HAVE ANY HABITS THAT YOU WISH TO CHANGE?

DATE : _____

23. Which parent are you closer to growing up and why?

DATE : _____

24. WHAT IS YOUR IDEA OF A PERFECT VACATION?

DATE : _____

25. WHAT'S YOUR THOUGHT ON ONLINE DATING?

DATE : _____

26. WHAT IS THE CRAZIEST THING YOU'VE EVER DONE AND WOULD YOU DO IT AGAIN?

DATE : _____

27. WHAT QUALITIES DO YOU ADMIRE ABOUT YOUR PARENTS?

DATE : _____

28. WHAT'S SOMETHING YOU CAN'T GO A DAY WITHOUT DOING?

DATE : _____

29. WHAT'S CLOSEST YOU'VE EVER COME TO BEING ARRESTED?

DATE : _____

30. IF YOU COULD HAVE ANYBODY ELSE'S LIFE, WHO'S WOULD YOU TAKE?

DATE : _____

31. WHAT FICTIONAL CHARACTER DO YOU MOST RELATE TO? WHY?

DATE : _____

32. WHAT IS YOUR BIGGEST IRRATIONAL FEAR?

DATE : _____

33. IF YOU COULD DO ONE THING WITHOUT SUFFERING THE CONSEQUENCES, WHAT WOULD YOU DO?

DATE : _____

34. WHAT IS THE STRANGEST DREAM YOU'VE EVER HAD?

DATE : _____

35. WHAT'S THE BEST LESSON YOU LEARNED FROM YOUR PARENTS?

DATE : _____

36. WOULD YOU RATHER BE CRAZY RICH, OR DEEPLY IN LOVE? WHY?

DATE : _____

37. When was the last time you really pushed yourself to your physical limits?

DATE : _____

38. WHAT'S THE THING YOU MOST WANT TO ACHIEVE BEFORE YOU DIE?

DATE : _____

39. WHO IS YOUR HERO GROWING UP? WHAT QUALITIES MAKE THEM YOUR CHOICE?

DATE : _____

40. WHAT'S YOUR FAVORITE MUSIC? HOW DOES IT MAKE YOU FEEL?

DATE : _____

41. WHAT KINDS OF PEOPLE DO YOU ENJOY MOST BEING AROUND?

DATE : _____

42. Do you think religion has been bad or good for the world?

DATE : _____

43. WHAT DO YOU DO FOR THE PEOPLE YOU LOVE THE MOST IN LIFE?

DATE : _____

44. WHAT DO YOU USUALLY DREAM ABOUT?

DATE : _____

45. WHAT DOES BEAUTY MEAN TO YOU?

DATE : _____

46. WHERE DO YOU THINK HAPPINESS COMES FROM?

DATE : _____

47. ARE YOUR PRIORITIES DIFFERENT NOW THAN WHAT THEY WERE IN THE PAST?

DATE : _____

48. If you had to get a tattoo right here right now, what would it be? Why?

DATE : _____

49. WHAT'S SOMETHING YOU TRY TO ACTIVELY AVOID IN LIFE?

DATE : _____

50. WHAT'S YOUR BIGGEST WEAKNESS?

DATE : _____

51. WHAT'S YOUR BIGGEST STRENGTH?

DATE : _____

52. WHAT QUALITIES DO YOU WISH YOU HAD THAT YOU DON'T?

DATE : _____

53. What's the biggest difference between you and your family?

DATE : _____

54. What makes you feel the most confident?

DATE : _____

55. WHO IN YOUR LIFE DO YOU WISH YOU MET SOONER?

DATE : _____

56. WHEN WAS THE FIRST TIME YOU KNEW THAT YOUR PARTNER WAS THE ONE YOU WANTED TO SPEND THE REST OF YOUR LIFE WITH?

DATE : _____

57. WHAT WAS YOUR FIRST IMPRESSION ABOUT YOUR PARTNER?

DATE : _____

58. WHAT IS THAT ONE DREAM YOU WANT YOUR PARTNER TO HELP YOU ACHIEVE?

DATE : _____

59. WHAT'S SOMETHING YOU WISH YOU DID TOGETHER MORE OFTEN?

DATE : _____

60. WHAT IS THE MOST CHERISHED THING OF YOUR DATING/MARRIED YEARS?

DATE : _____

61. HOW FREQUENTLY WOULD YOU LIKE TO GO OUT ON A DATE WITH YOUR PARTNER?

DATE : _____

62. WHAT ARE THE DIFFERENT WAYS IN WHICH YOU WANT YOUR PARTNER TO EXPRESS FOR YOU?

DATE : _____

63. WHAT HOBBY YOU COULD TAKE UP TOGETHER?

DATE : _____

64. WAS THERE ANY INSTANCE WHEN IT WAS HARD FOR YOU TO OPEN-UP TO YOUR PARTNER?

DATE : _____

65. HOW WOULD YOU LIKE TO SPEND YOUR DAYS TOGETHER AFTER YOU AGE?

DATE : _____

66. WHAT TEACHING OR QUALITY OF YOUR PARENTS DO YOU APPRECIATE?

DATE : _____

67. HOW CAN YOU HELP YOUR PARTNER BE CONFIDENT ABOUT YOUR RELATIONSHIP?

DATE : _____

68. WHAT ARE YOU THE MOST GRATEFUL FOR IN YOUR CURRENT RELATIONSHIP?

DATE : _____

69. WHAT WAS YOUR AMBITION AS A TEENAGER?

Date: _____

70. What's your favorite thing about your relationship?

DATE : _____

71. WHAT DO YOU LOOK FORWARD TO ABOUT HAVING KIDS?

DATE : _____

72. WHAT SHOULD A HEALTHY RELATIONSHIP PROVIDE FOR THE PEOPLE IN IT?

DATE : _____

73. HAVE YOU OVERCOME ANY OF YOUR PHOBIAS? IF YES, HOW?

DATE : _____

74. WHAT IS YOUR IDEA OF A PERFECT DATE?

DATE : _____

75. WHAT IS THAT ONE BAD AND DIFFICULT HABIT YOU WANT TO BREAK?

DATE : _____

76. WHAT'S YOUR FAVORITE NON-PHYSICAL QUALITY ABOUT YOUR PARTNER?

DATE : _____

77. WHAT'S YOUR FAVORITE PLACE THAT YOU SHOULD GO TO TOGETHER, AND WHY?

DATE : _____

78. WHAT WAS THE DUMBEST THING YOU EVER DID?

DATE : _____

79. IF YOU HAD ONE DAY LEFT ON EARTH, WHAT WOULD YOU WANT TO DO?

DATE : _____

80. IS THERE ANYTHING YOU'VE ALWAYS WONDERED ABOUT YOUR PARTNER, BUT HAVE HESITATED TO ASK?

DATE : _____

81. WHAT DO YOU LOVE THE MOST ABOUT YOUR RELATIONSHIP?

DATE : _____

82. WHAT'S THE LAST BOOK YOU READ AND REALLY ENJOYED? WHAT WAS IT ABOUT?

DATE : _____

83. WHAT DO YOU THINK ABOUT ASTROLOGY AND HOROSCOPES?

DATE : _____

84. WHAT WOULD YOU SAY IS YOUR PARTNER'S WORST TRAIT?

DATE : _____

85. WHAT WOULD YOU SAY IS YOUR PARTNER'S BEST TRAIT?

DATE : _____

86. WHAT'S SOMETHING YOU'VE TRIED THAT YOU THOUGHT YOU'D HATE BUT ACTUALLY END UP LIKING?

DATE : _____

87. WHICH COUNTRY WOULD YOU LIKE TO VISIT TOGETHER?

DATE : _____

88. IF YOU COULD RELIVE ONE DAY OF YOUR LIFE, WHICH DAY WOULD YOU PICK?

DATE : _____

89. WHAT IS ONE THING YOU THINK COULD MAKE YOUR RELATIONSHIP STRONGER?

DATE : _____

90. WHAT DO YOU THINK COULD BE IMPROVED IN YOUR RELATIONSHIP?

DATE : _____

91. WHAT SCARES YOU MOST WHEN IT COMES TO LOVE?

DATE : _____

92. WHAT THING DO YOU HATE ABOUT YOURSELF THAT YOUR PARTNER LOVE?

DATE : _____

93. HOW DID YOU THINK THIS RELATIONSHIP WOULD BE WHEN YOU STARTED DATING?

DATE : _____

94. WHAT IS THAT ONE DREAM YOU WANT YOUR PARTNER TO HELP YOU ACHIEVE?

DATE : _____

95. WHAT DO YOU HOPE TO ACHIEVE TOGETHER IN THE NEXT 3 YEARS?

DATE : _____

96. WHAT PERSONAL FLAW THAT YOU'D FIX, IF YOU COULD?

DATE : _____

97. DO YOU BELIEVE IN FATE AND WHY?

DATE : _____

98. WHAT DO YOU THINK ABOUT OPEN RELATIONSHIP?

DATE : _____

99. WHAT'S ONE SECRET YOU'VE ALWAYS WANTED TO TELL YOUR PARTNER BUT HAVEN'T?

DATE : _____

100. When have you felt like you were living life to the fullest?

DATE : _____

101. WHAT ARE YOUR HOPES FOR YOUR CURRENT RELATIONSHIP GOING IN FRONT?

CPSIA information can be obtained
at www.ICGtesting.com
Printed in the USA
BVHW041019300122
627564BV00017B/431